FREEDOM FORCES

☆U.S. AIR FORCE:☆

ABSOLUTE AIRPOWER

Sneed B. Collard III

Rourke
Educational Media
rourkeeducationalmedia.com

www.rourkeeducationalmedia.com

PHOTO CREDITS: Cover: Metal texture © Andrey_Kuzmin, main photo courtesy of the U.S. Air Force; back cover and title page: flag © SFerdon; Pages 4/5: U.S. Air Force photo/Tech. Sgt. Fernando Serna); Pages 6/7: US Army, USAF; Pages 8/9: US Military, USAF; Pages 10/11: Courtesy of the Unites States Air Force Historical Research Agency; Pages 12/13: USAF, US Army; Pages 14/15 ship © Songquan Deng, logo: USAF; Pages 16/17 © USAF, NASA; Pages 18/19 USAF, page 18 bomb: © Sturmvogel 66; Pages 20: USAF; Page 21 © tomas del amo; Pages 22/23: USAF; Pages 24/25: USAF, SSGT Ernest H. Sealing; Pages 26/27 © US Military, USAF; Pages 28/29 background photo © Ensuper, Wright Brothers photo © John T. Daniels for, other photos: USAF Pages 30/31 folder art © McVectors, logo: USAF

Edited by Precious McKenzie

Designed and Produced by Blue Door Publishing, FL

Library of Congress Cataloging-in-Publication Data

U.S. Air Force: Absolute Air Power / Sneed B. Collard III
  p. cm. -- (Freedom Forces)
  ISBN 978-1-62169-920-0 (hard cover) (alk. paper)
  ISBN 978-1-62169-815-9 (soft cover)
  ISBN 978-1-62717-024-6 (e-book)
Library of Congress Control Number: 2013938872

Rourke Educational Media
Printed in the United States of America,
North Mankato, Minnesota

Also Available as:
ROURKE'S
e-Books

Rourke
Educational Media
rourkeeducationalmedia.com
customerservice@rourkeeducationalmedia.com
PO Box 643328 Vero Beach, Florida 32964

TABLE OF CONTENTS

F-16A Fighting Falcons, F-15C, and F-15E Eagles fly over burning oil fields during Desert Storm.

4

CHAPTER ONE

PRECISE DESTRUCTION

On January 17, 1991, the United States and more than three dozen other nations attacked the country of Iraq. Their mission? To dislodge Iraqi forces from the tiny country of Kuwait. Six months earlier, without warning, Iraqi dictator Saddam Hussein ordered the invasion of Kuwait. Iraq seized Kuwait's precious oil fields, posing a threat to the entire region. Now, the United States and its allies hoped to liberate Kuwait and dismantle Iraq's war machine.

Iraq fielded one of the world's most powerful military forces. U.S. experts worried that the war would lead to thousands of American and **allied** casualties. Beginning at 3 a.m. on the morning of January 17, however, a massive force of 668 aircraft attacked Iraq. They unleashed a terrifying barrage of bombs and missiles that destroyed targets with astounding accuracy.

The Su-25, like this one destroyed during Operation Desert Storm, was nicknamed *Gratch* meaning The *Rook* by the Russians. This comes from a bird and its ability to get food in hard to reach spots. Similarly, the SU-25 can destroy targets in hard to reach places.

This B-52 heavy bomber joined stealth aircraft, attack fighters, helicopters, and many other aircraft in attacking Iraq during the first Gulf War.

Within hours, the allies knocked out much of Iraq's communications network, air force, and defenses. In the days that followed, allied aircraft pulverized Iraq's ground forces with equal ferocity.

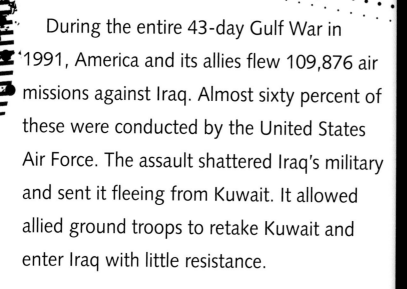

During the entire 43-day Gulf War in 1991, America and its allies flew 109,876 air missions against Iraq. Almost sixty percent of these were conducted by the United States Air Force. The assault shattered Iraq's military and sent it fleeing from Kuwait. It allowed allied ground troops to retake Kuwait and enter Iraq with little resistance.

This 2,000 pound (907 kilogram) Mark 84 bomb is capable of forming a crater 50 feet (15.24 meters) wide and 36 feet (11 meters) deep.

Thanks to the dominance of the United States Air Force and other allied forces, only 148 allied troops lost their lives in combat during the war.

This overwhelming victory sent two important messages to the nations of the world. First, in modern armed conflict, whoever controlled the skies controlled the battlefield. Second, no military on Earth could match the power and precision of the United States Air Force.

CHAPTER TWO

A NEW BATTLEFRONT

Air combat, like those used during the Gulf War, didn't become possible until the invention of the airplane in the early 1900s. Just ten short years after the invention of the airplane, militaries began to use airplanes for combat.

In 1909, the U.S. Army bought the world's first airplane for military use from the Wright brothers. Even after the start of World War I, most military minds thought that airplanes would only ever be used to observe enemy troop movements.

The first fighter planes were built with a wooden frame, covered with fabric, and limited to about 100 miles per hour (160.93 kilometers per hour).

World War I heralded the first widespread use of aircraft. British, French, and German pilots engaged in thrilling **dog fights** to shoot each other down. Opposing nations also began dropping bombs from airplanes, but these rarely came close to their targets. By the time the United States entered World War I in 1918, its aircraft industry had fallen far behind Europe's. The birth of real American air power would have to wait for the next major war.

The Douglas A-20 Havoc night fighter was made for high altitude bombing. Its first flight was on January 23, 1939.

In World War II, American factories operated around the clock to build aircraft to defeat Germany and Japan. American and British fighters took on German Messerschmitt and Japanese Zeros in battles to control the skies. Wave after wave of Allied bombers dropped more than two million tons of bombs on enemy cities and factories. Other airplanes transported cargo and troops as they battled to defeat German and Japanese forces.

The Martin B-10 was the first all-metal monoplane bomber to go into regular use by the United States Army Air Corps.

This B-29 heavy bomber got its name from Enola Gay Tibbets, the mother of the pilot who selected the aircraft while it was still on the assembly line.

One of the most famous aircraft of World War II was the B-29 heavy bomber, used in the war to defeat Japan. A B-29, named the Enola Gay, dropped the atomic bomb on the Japanese city of Hiroshima, helping to bring a quick end to the war.

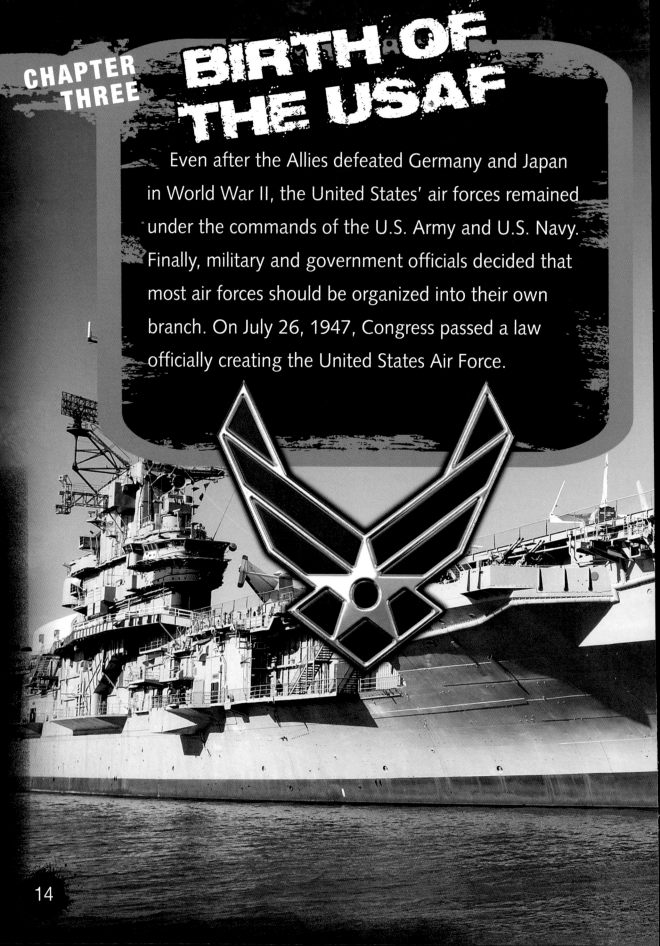

CHAPTER THREE

BIRTH OF THE USAF

Even after the Allies defeated Germany and Japan in World War II, the United States' air forces remained under the commands of the U.S. Army and U.S. Navy. Finally, military and government officials decided that most air forces should be organized into their own branch. On July 26, 1947, Congress passed a law officially creating the United States Air Force.

Despite the creation of the United States Air Force, the U.S. Navy retains control over its own aircraft carriers and warplanes. The Army, Marine Corps, and Coast Guard also operate their own aircraft, mostly helicopters.

Since its official creation, the USAF has played a decisive role in the Korean War, the Vietnam War, both Gulf wars, the war in Afghanistan, and countless smaller conflicts. During and after the **Cold War**, it manned long-range missiles capable of delivering a nuclear attack on the Soviet Union and other enemies. Today, the mission of the USAF is "to fly, fight and win...in air, space and **cyberspace**."

The USAF has produced no shortage of heroes, both men and women. One of the most famous is Edwin, or Buzz, Aldrin. Buzz flew sixty-six combat missions during the Korean War before becoming a NASA astronaut in 1963. On July 20, 1969, he landed the first manned spacecraft on the Moon and, following Neil Armstrong, became the second person to set foot on the lunar surface.

Buzz Aldrin

THE U.S. AIR FORCE

★ controls air space in any military conflict

★ defends America and its allies from attack

★ launches precision attacks anywhere, anytime in the world with minimum casualties

★ transports troops, commanders, weapons, and equipment

★ collects and protects information vital to military commanders and our nation

★ provides humanitarian aid after natural disasters

The F-117 Night Hawk is a single-seat, twin-engine stealth ground-attack aircraft widely publicized for its role in the Persian Gulf War.

The world's first laser-guided bomb, the BOLT-117 paved the way for laser guided bombs and changed the course of modern warfare as we know it.

CHAPTER FOUR

TODAY'S AIR FORCE

To accomplish its mission, the United States Air Force uses an astounding array of weapons and equipment. These range from advanced fighter aircraft and radar systems to computers and space satellites. The USAF operates almost fifty kinds of aircraft alone. Some of the most awe-inspiring are its **stealth** fighters and bombers.

A large slice of the success in the Gulf War can be given to the stealth F-117 Night Hawk attack aircraft. The Night Hawk featured a special design and technology that made it almost invisible to enemy radar. This allowed it to easily slip behind enemy lines. The F-117 was equipped with highly accurate **smart bombs** that improved accuracy and reduced civilian casualties. A wing of ten F-117s dropped the very first bombs on Baghdad during the first Gulf War.

An F117 Night Hawk dropping a GBU-28 guided bomb.

After the Gulf War, the Air Force rolled out another deadly addition to its stealth arsenal, the B-2 Spirit bomber. Originally designed to carry nuclear weapons, the B-2 first saw action in 1999, attacking Serbian targets during the Kosovo War. The B-2s also went to war in Afghanistan and, more recently, in Libya. Currently, the Air Force is introducing its newest stealth aircraft, the F-22 Raptor, to replace the retired F-117.

B-2 Spirit Bomber

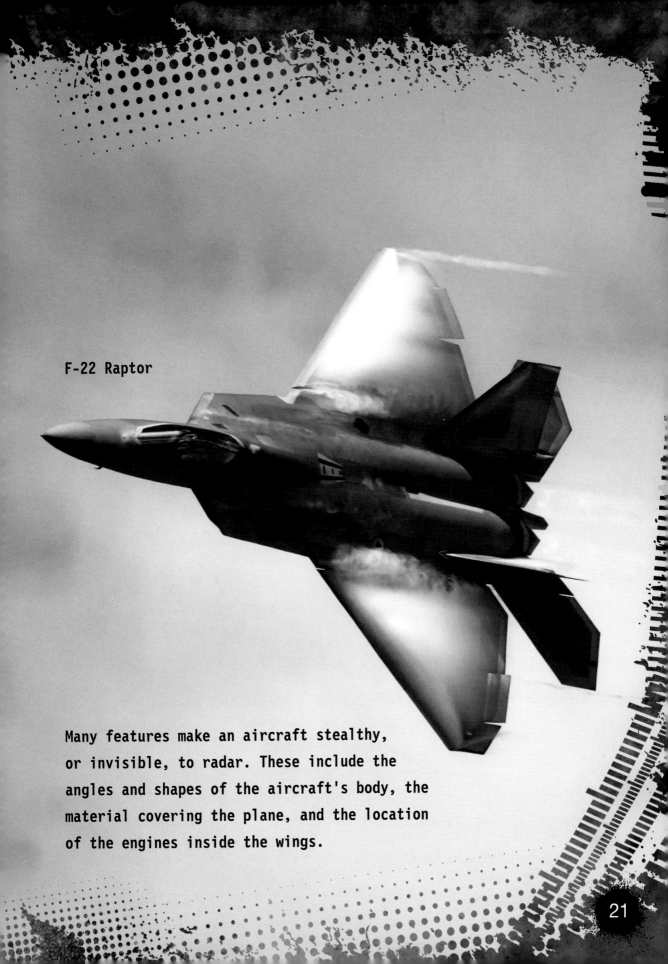

F-22 Raptor

Many features make an aircraft stealthy, or invisible, to radar. These include the angles and shapes of the aircraft's body, the material covering the plane, and the location of the engines inside the wings.

21

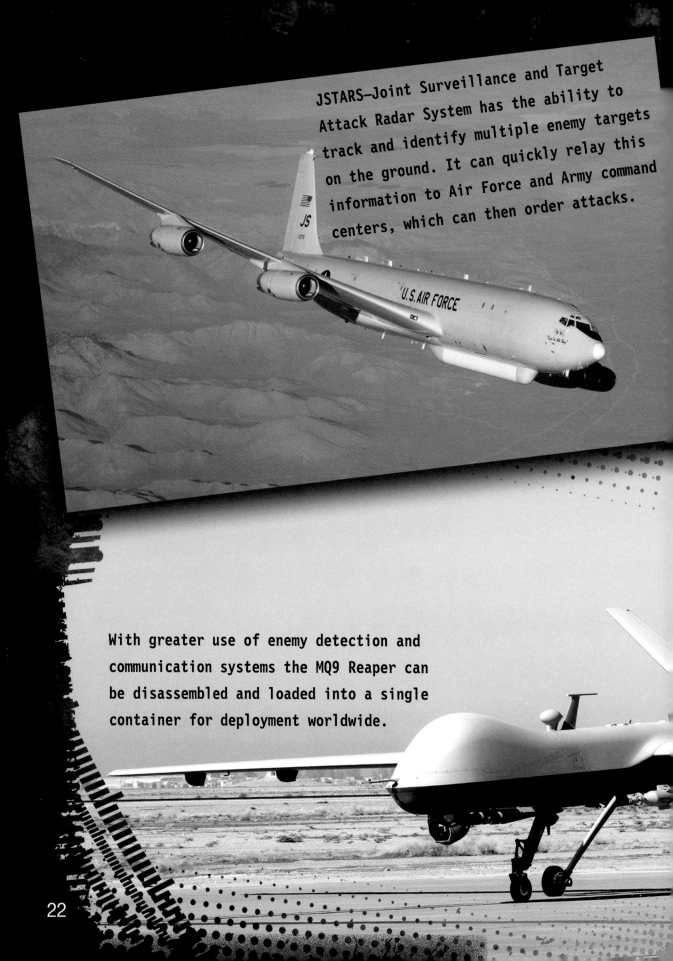

JSTARS—Joint Surveillance and Target Attack Radar System has the ability to track and identify multiple enemy targets on the ground. It can quickly relay this information to Air Force and Army command centers, which can then order attacks.

With greater use of enemy detection and communication systems the MQ9 Reaper can be disassembled and loaded into a single container for deployment worldwide.

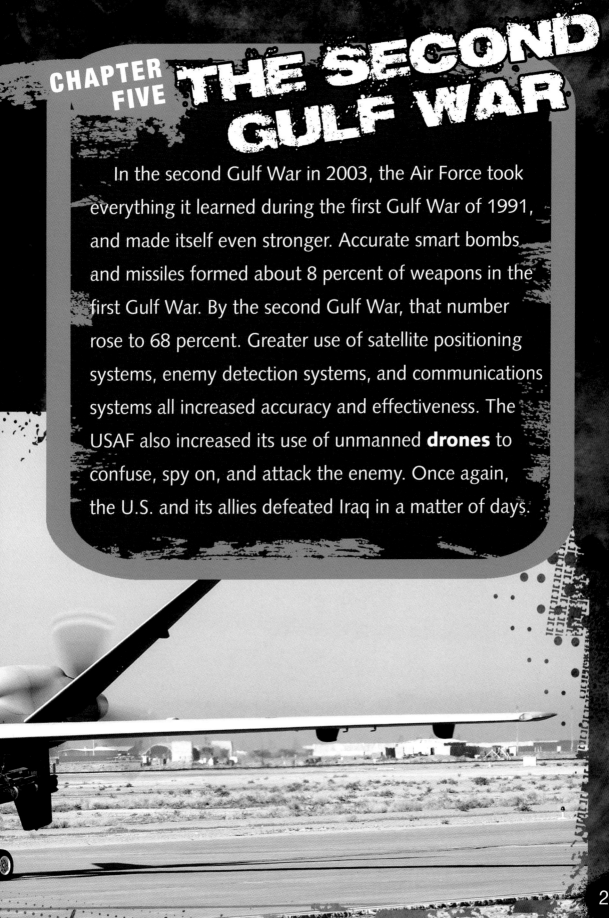

CHAPTER FIVE
THE SECOND GULF WAR

In the second Gulf War in 2003, the Air Force took everything it learned during the first Gulf War of 1991, and made itself even stronger. Accurate smart bombs and missiles formed about 8 percent of weapons in the first Gulf War. By the second Gulf War, that number rose to 68 percent. Greater use of satellite positioning systems, enemy detection systems, and communications systems all increased accuracy and effectiveness. The USAF also increased its use of unmanned **drones** to confuse, spy on, and attack the enemy. Once again, the U.S. and its allies defeated Iraq in a matter of days.

WAR ON TERROR

CHAPTER SIX

Since the second Gulf War, U.S. military efforts have focused on fighting terrorists in Afghanistan and elsewhere. Air Force Combat Controllers play a key role in these operations. Working alone or with **Navy SEALs** and other special forces, Combat Controllers quietly slip into enemy territory. They set up communications, conduct surveillance, and coordinate air attacks on enemy forces.

An F-15E Strike Eagle launches heat decoys during a close air support mission over Afghanistan on December 15, 2008.

24

Part of the Combat Controller's job is to establish landing zones for incoming troops, and to coordinate air traffic over combat zones.

25

Today, the United States Air Force is the largest, most advanced, and most battle-tested air power on Earth. It has to be. With constant threats from terrorists and hostile nations, the Air Force has to be prepared to face a wide variety of situations. In the last decade, the USAF has also delivered critical food, medicine, and transportation following devastating earthquakes in Japan, Haiti, and Indonesia. USAF men and women proudly risk their lives not only to protect us, but to help people in need.

The United States Air Force doesn't just use its resources to serve the military mission, it also uses them to serve mankind.

THE USAF OFFERS CAREERS IN A HUGE VARIETY OF FIELDS. SOME OF THE MOST POPULAR ARE:

★ pilot
★ pararescue
★ combat control
★ space operations
★ explosive ordinance disposal
★ chaplain
★ family medicine
★ law
★ aircraft maintenance
★ air traffic control

To learn more, visit http://www.airforce.com/careers/

A combat controller providing air traffic control.

TIMELINE

1861-1863:
Use of air balloons to follow troop movements during Civil War.

1914-1918 (World War I):
First large-scale use of military aircraft in combat.

1947:
United States Air Force officially created.

1903:
Wright brothers successfully fly first engine-powered airplane.

1939-1945 (World War II):
Aircraft play decisive role in defeat of Germany and Japan.

1959:
Air Force puts first intercontinental ballistic missile into service during the Cold War.

1965:
USAF launches first air strikes against North Vietnam during Vietnam War.

1980:
First women graduate from the United States Air Force Academy.

2001:
Operation Enduring Freedom, America's war on terrorism, begins.

1978:
Air Force launches first satellite in its GPS (global positioning system) network.

1991:
First Gulf War.

2010:
USAF takes part in Operation Unified Response to help victims of Haiti's devastating earthquake.

SHOW WHAT YOU KNOW

1. When was the official U.S. Air Force created?
2. Summarize the mission of the U.S. Air Force.
3. How did the U.S. and its allies work against Iraq?
4. Besides defense missions, describe the other types of missions that the Air Force handles.
5. If you could have any career in the U.S. Air Force, what would it be? Why?

GLOSSARY

allied (AL-ide): belonging to the United States and countries fighting with it

Cold War (KOLD WOR): the build up of weapons between the United States and the former Soviet Union from the 1950s until the 1980s

cyberspace (SIE-bur-spase): having to do with computer networks and communications

dog fights (DOG fites): air battles between two or more opposing aircraft

drones (dronz): unmanned aircraft

Navy SEALS (nay-VEE SEELZ): the Navy's special forces that conduct secret, often dangerous, military operations

smart bombs (SMART BOMZ): bombs that use laser, satellite, or camera guidance systems to steer toward their targets

stealth (STELTH): in the military, aircraft or other vehicles that are almost invisible to radar

Index

Websites to Visit

http://www.airforce.com/

http://www.pbs.org/wgbh/pages/frontline/gulf/

http://www.nationalmuseum.af.mil/index.asp

About the Author

Sneed B. Collard III has written more than 65 books for young people including the award-winning books *Science Warriors—The Battle Against Invasive Species*, *Pocket Babies and Other Amazing Marsupials*, and *The World Famous Miles City Bucking Horse Sale*. His popular novels include *Dog Sense*, *Hangman's Gold*, and *Cartwheel—A Sequel to Double Eagle*. Watch book trailers for Sneed's books on his YouTube channel, and learn more about him at www.sneedbcollardiii.com.

Meet The Author!
www.meetREMauthors.com